# Contents

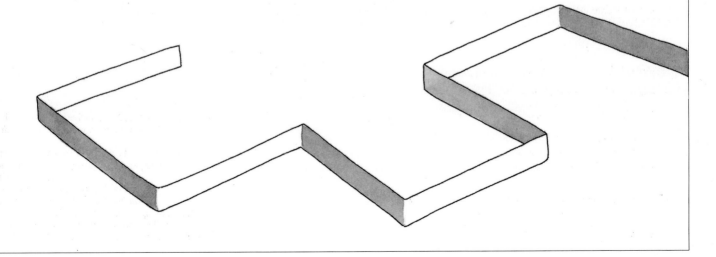

# Calculate it!

In 1780 an American slave called Thomas Fuller was asked to say how long he had lived, in seconds. At the time, he was 70 years and 17days old.

It took him just 90 seconds to work out the answer in his head. The person who had asked the question used pencil and paper and took much longer to come up with an answer. The two answers disagreed, the pencil and paper solution was less than Thomas Fuller's. Fuller pointed out that his was the correct solution, because in his mental calculation he had also included the extra days in the leap years.

Thomas Fuller was born in Africa in 1710. In 1724 he was taken prisoner and transported to Virginia in the USA as a slave. He was never taught to read or write, but he did have amazing abilities with mental arithmetic. In his head he was able to do such things as multiply two nine-digit numbers together and work out how many grains of wheat there were in a given weight.

## In your head

How quickly can you work out how long you have lived in seconds? Can you work it out in your head? ... on paper? ... or using a calculator?

Today we use calculators to speed up calculations. They also bring difficult mathematical puzzles and problems within our reach.

Throughout this book you will find it useful to have a calculator as well as pencil and paper on hand, to help you in finding solutions.

Though many of the puzzles in this book may have one unique answer, that does not necessarily mean there is only one way of arriving at that solution. The most important thing is to develop your own ways of solving puzzles and problems. The variety of methods used to solve a puzzle can be as interesting as the puzzle itself.

## Divided

I have divided a one-digit number by another one-digit number and the answer on my calculator is 0.4 What were my two numbers?

I have divided another one-digit number by a one-digit number and the answer is 0.2222222 What were my two numbers?

*Is there a way to find the answer quickly?* Try inventing similar problems for friends to solve. If one-digit problems are easy, go on to larger numbers.

# HOW PUZZLING

*Charles Snape and Heather Scott*

The right of the
University of Cambridge
to print and sell
all manner of books
was granted by
Henry VIII in 1534.
The University has printed
and published continuously
since 1584.

**Cambridge University Press**
Cambridge
New York  Port Chester
Melbourne  Sydney

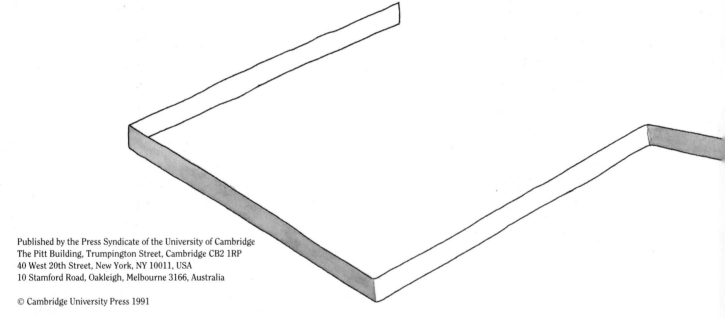

Published by the Press Syndicate of the University of Cambridge
The Pitt Building, Trumpington Street, Cambridge CB2 1RP
40 West 20th Street, New York, NY 10011, USA
10 Stamford Road, Oakleigh, Melbourne 3166, Australia

© Cambridge University Press 1991

First published 1991

Printed in Great Britain by  Scotprint Ltd.

British Library cataloguing-in-publication data
Snape, Charles
    How puzzling.
    1. Mathematical puzzles
    I. Title II. Scott, Heather
    793. 74

Library of Congress cataloging-in-publication data

ISBN 0 521 35673 3 paperback

Design and artwork by Juliet & Charles Snape Limited
Illustrations by Juliet Snape and Sean MacGarry

The authors and the publisher would like to thank
the following for permission to reproduce
copyright material:
The Rhind Papyrus (page 6) reproduced by Courtesy of
the Trustees of the British Museum.
Egyptian Labyrinth. Restored plan (Canina) (page 32)
from Mazes and Labyrinths by W.H. Matthews
published by Longmans, Green and Co, London 1922.

## A few keys

Imagine that you can only use the following keys on your calculator:

*What numbers between 1 and 50 can you make with them?* Did you make these numbers by using the smallest number of key presses possible?

You can make 18 by pressing twelve keys:

but

also makes 18 and you only press six keys.

You can make similar problems for yourself by changing the numbers and the signs that you are allowed to use.

## Multiplication chains

Start with a number          372
Multiply the digits together
3 x 7 x 2 = 42
Keep multiplying          4 x 2 = 8
until you are left with only one digit.
So 372 took two steps to finish.

*Which number below 500 takes the greatest number of steps to finish?*

## Taxing island

On a remote island of Egret, the ruling elders have a special system of taxation. Islanders are taxed such that they pay the same percentage in taxes as they earn in thousands. So for example someone who earns 4 000 Nazricks would pay 4% of these earnings to the island, and someone who earns 75 000 Nazricks would pay 75% of these earnings to the island.

*What amount of money would you like to earn so that you are left with the most money after you have paid your taxes?*

## Sequences

You can make up rules to generate sequences of numbers. Sometimes the sequences end up in a particular place. The following two problems are about repeating rules. Try to see what is happening and predict what will happen for any start numbers combined with any rule.

| | |
|---|---|
| Work with one number to start with | 7 |
| Divide your number by 3 and then add 1 | 3.3333333 |
| Divide your new number by 3 and then add 1 to get the next number | 2.1111111 |

Keep repeating the rule until you notice something. Investigate with different starting numbers and the same rule. Try different rules.

Start with two different numbers

To get the next two numbers quarter Y column number...

$$\begin{array}{cc} X & Y \\ 3 \;_{(5+3)} \quad _{(\div 4)} & 8 \\ 2 & 8 \\ 2 & 9 \\ 2.25 & 10 \\ 2.5 & 10.75 \end{array}$$

... and add 3 to the difference between X and Y

Predict what will happen with different starting numbers in each of the columns. Predict what will happen with different rules for each of the columns.

# Papyrus puzzles

## A quantity and a quarter of it are together 15. How much is it?

The problem above comes from one of the oldest pieces of written mathematics which has been discovered so far. It can be found on a papyrus scroll that was written, over 3500 years ago, by an Egyptian scribe called Ahmes. The scroll is called the 'Rhind Papyrus' after the antique collector, Henry Rhind, who bought it in 1858 in the Egyptian town of Luxor. Our knowledge of ancient Egyptian mathematics comes mainly from this scroll, which you can see today in the British Museum in London.

Ahmes, the writer, tells us that it is not his own work on the scroll. He explains that it comes from a scroll which was written 200 years earlier in about 1850 BC.

The scroll which was originally 30.5cm wide and 550cm long (1ft x 18ft) contains mathematical problems, exercises and puzzles. No one is sure for whom it was written; it could have been a type of text book for trainee accountants or tax collectors, or maybe even a 'text book' for school children.

## Egyptian multiplication

The Rhind Papyrus shows us the way that the Egyptians, in 1650 BC, used to multiply numbers together. They used to solve problems like 15 x 16 by using a method of doubling and adding until they had the right answer:

$$1 \times 16 \text{ or } (1 \text{ lot of } 16) = 16$$
$$\text{so } 2 \times 16 \text{ or } (2 \text{ lots of } 16) = 32$$
$$\text{so } 4 \times 16 \text{ or } (4 \text{ lots of } 16) = 64$$
$$\text{so } 8 \times 16 \text{ or } (8 \text{ lots of } 16) = 128$$

Altogether this comes to 15 lots of sixteen so if you add up all the answers, 15 x 16 = 240.

You may like to do the following using the Egyptian way of multiplying numbers together.

| 19 x 19 | 24 x 29 | 6 x 46 |
|---|---|---|

| 8 x 7 | 11 x 15 | 13 x 22 |
|---|---|---|

*Do you think that this is a good method? Will it always work?*

This is a section of the Rhind Papyrus. The writing on it is in hieratic script which was a development from the earlier Egyptian Hieroglyphics.

fractions which you get when you divide 2 by any odd number between 3 and 101. This is probably because it would take you a lot of time to work them out from scratch each time they were needed.

Here is the beginning of that table:

$\frac{2}{3}$ = ⁊

$\frac{2}{5} = \frac{1}{3} + \frac{1}{15}$

$\frac{2}{7} = \frac{1}{4} + \frac{1}{28}$

Here are some examples of how the Egyptians would build up their fractions:

| | | | |
|---|---|---|---|
| First find the largest unit fraction that will go into it | $\frac{5}{9} = \frac{1}{2}$ | + something | (both 9 and 2 go into 18) |
| | $\frac{10}{18} = \frac{9}{18}$ | + something | |
| | $\frac{5}{9} = \frac{1}{2}$ | + $\frac{1}{18}$ | |
| | $\frac{2}{9} = \frac{1}{5}$ | + something | (what number will 9 and 5 |
| | $\frac{10}{45} = \frac{9}{45}$ | + something | go into without any |
| | $\frac{2}{9} = \frac{1}{5}$ | + $\frac{1}{45}$ | remainder?) |

*Using the Egyptians' method is it possible to build up all the fractions $\frac{2}{5}$ , $\frac{2}{7}$ , $\frac{2}{9}$ and so on up to $\frac{2}{101}$ , with just two unit fractions?*

*What is the minimum number of unit fractions needed to build up the fractions $\frac{3}{4}$ , $\frac{3}{5}$ , $\frac{3}{7}$ , and so on up to $\frac{3}{101}$ ? Investigate with other fractions.*

## Problem 79

In the 79th problem on the Rhind Papyrus Ahmes poses the following question:

Seven houses each have seven cats. The seven cats each kill seven mice. Each of the mice would have eaten seven ears of wheat. Each ear of wheat would have produced seven measures of flour. How many measures of flour were saved by the cats?

## Egyptian fractions

The Egyptians only used unit fractions in their mathematics. A unit fraction is one which has a '1' on the top. For example: $\frac{1}{2}$ , $\frac{1}{8}$ , $\frac{1}{4}$ , $\frac{1}{37}$ are all 'unit' fractions. There was one exception to this rule and that was the symbol ⁊ which stands for $\frac{2}{3}$ . The first part of the Rhind Papyrus gives us a table of the combinations of unit fractions which are needed to make up all the

## PS to problem 79

If you have worked out how many measures of flour were saved by the cats, you might like to solve the following problem in this eighteenth century nursery rhyme. You might notice the similarity with Ahmes' problem!

As I was going to St. Ives,
I met a man with seven wives.
Every wife had seven sacks.
Every sack had seven cats.
Every cat had seven kits.
Kits, cats, sacks and wives,
How many were going to St. Ives?

# Problems of Babylon

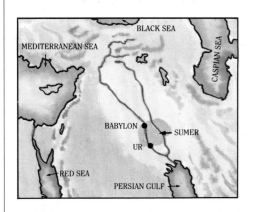

The Babylonians lived in the Mesopotamian valley in the Middle East. Their civilisation lasted for about 1400 years between 2000 BC and 600 BC.

We are able to find out about the type of mathematics which the Babylonians did because they used to write in 'cuneiform script' by pressing triangular shaped wedges into clay tablets.
These cuneiform tablets were then baked until they were hard to give a permanent record of their work, which we are able to decipher and read today.

The following is an old Babylonian problem.

## Silver and sisters
There are eight sisters who have to share $1\frac{2}{3}$ minas of silver between them. Each sister in turn receives more than the previous sister and the difference between the quantities that each successive sister receives is the same. If the second sister gets six shekels, what is the common difference?

A talent is worth 60 minas

A mina is worth 60 shekels

A shekel is worth 60 grains

## Babylonian Number System
The Babylonian number system is interesting for many reasons. They used 60 as a base, probably because it was useful for astronomical calculations and the practical problems concerned with weights and measures. This base 60 system has certainly stood the test of time as it is still frequently used today. *How many seconds are there in one minute? How many minutes in one hour? How many degrees are there in one full turn?*

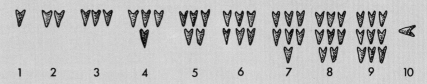

1  2  3  4  5  6  7  8  9  10

Using the system the number 90 would be represented by

1 lot of 60 and 3 lots of 10 makes 90.

Can you match the questions with the answers?

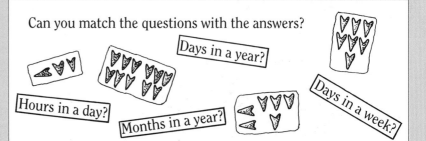

Days in a year?

Hours in a day?

Months in a year?

Days in a week?

## Babylonian square

What is the length of the side of the square? If the area of a square less its side is

14 lots of 60 and 3 lots of 10 (which equals 870 in our decimal system).

In the Babylonian system the value of the wedge depended upon its position. Because there was no symbol for zero this created a problem with knowing exactly how much the number was worth. For example ...

does  stand for

3 lots of $(60)^2$ and 2 lots of 60 which would make 10920 as we know it?

or does it stand for 3 lots of 60 and 2 which makes 182 as we know it?

Because the Babylonians also used the same symbols for fractions it could also stand for 3 lots of 1 and 2 lots of $\frac{1}{60}$ which makes $3\frac{1}{30}$ as we know it. With no zero you needed to be able to understand the problem being posed so that you would know how large the numbers should be.

## Measuring land
The Babylonians used practical methods to measure land. They would cut up shapes and turn them into rectangles.

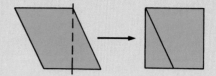

To turn a parallelogram into a rectangle you only need to make one cut along the dotted line, as shown. *How many cuts would you need to turn each of the following shapes into rectangles?*

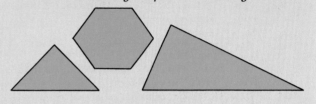

## Babylonian hand
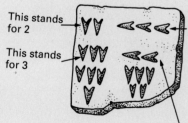
A quater of the width of an object and one length, added together make 7 hands. Also, the length and the width added together make 10 hands. *What are the length and the width?*

## Investigating reciprocals
Ancient cuneiform tablets have been found which show tables of numbers constructed by the Babylonian mathematicians. One of the most fascinating to investigate is the table of reciprocal numbers. Here is the beginning of this table:

This stands for 2

This stands for 3

This stands for 30 sixtieths ($\frac{30}{60}$) which is what you get when you divide 1 by 2 ($\frac{1}{2}$) in base 60.

This stands for 20 sixtieths which is what you get when you divide 1 by 3 in base 60.

In our number system (base 10) the reciprocal of 3 is $\frac{1}{3}$ or 1 divided by 3. In the Babylonian system the reciprocal of 3 is still $\frac{1}{3}$ but you have to do the division in base 60.

$$\overset{0,20}{3)\overline{1,^60}}$$

3 into 1 won't go. So the 1 is changed to 60 sixtieths. 3 into 60 goes 20 times.

*How would you carry on the Babylonian table of reciprocals?*

*Are all the numbers easy to work out?*

*What differences are there between reciprocals in our decimal system (base 10) and the Babylonian sexigesimal system (base 60)?*

# Pi and paradoxes

## Puzzling pi

The Greek letter π (pi) stands for the number that you need to multiply the length of the diameter of a circle by to find that the circle's circumference. π is always the same no matter how large or small a circle is.

In ancient civilisations, mathematicians found that a circle's circumference was three and a bit times its diameter. The exact value of the bit has proved impossible to find.

3.1416 is the approximate value of π that we accept today, but computers have calculated it to over one hundred thousand decimal places. Yet, the fact is, there is no exact value of π. The area of a circle is found by multiplying the length of the radius of a circle by itself and then multiplying the answer by π. This can be written as r x r x π or πr².

One of the problems on the Rhind Papyrus shows us that the ancient Egyptians must have had a rule for finding the area of a circle.

---

Problem 50 is about the area of a circular field with a diameter of 9 units. The problem says that it would have exactly the same area as a square field whose sides were each 8 units.

9 units / 8 units

*If this is true, what value for π must the Egyptians have used?*

Ancient Chinese mathematicians have told us that the area of a circle can be found by working out $\frac{3}{4}$ of the area of the square drawn on the diameter of that circle. *If this is true, what would the Ancient Chinese value for π have been?*

Is the area of the circle three quarters of the square?

In the sixth century Brahmagupta, an Indian mathematician, used two values for π. He called 3 the 'practical' value and √10 the 'neat' value. *How far away from the real π are these two numbers?*

---

In 430 BC the people of Athens were being ravaged by a plague. The Oracle at Delos was asked how this plague could be stopped. It replied that the altar of Apollo, which was an exact cube, must be built to exactly double its present size. The Athenians quickly set about making it twice as long as the old altar. The plague continued. Again the Oracle was consulted. It replied, "the new altar should also be an exact cube and the volume of this cube should be exactly twice the volume of the old one."

## The Delian problem

The Delian problem arises from two old legends. The first is based on the story above. The second tells us about King Minos of Crete getting a tomb ready for Glancus. When Minos found out that each side of the tomb was only 100 feet he said, "Small indeed is the tomb thou hast chosen for a Royal burial. Let it be double, and thou shalt not miss that fair form if thou quickly doublest each side of the tomb."

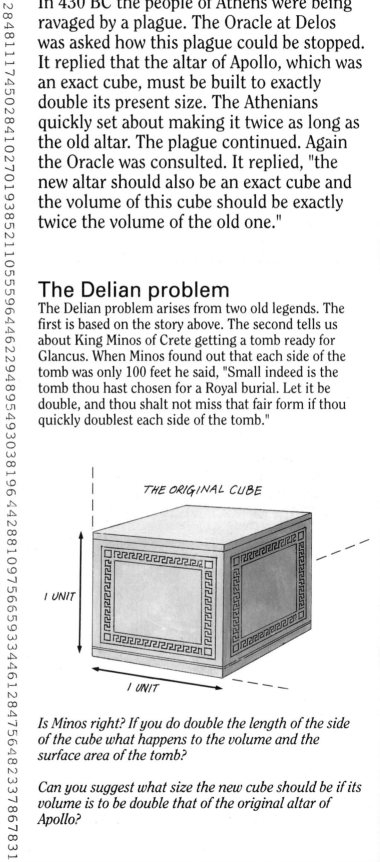

THE ORIGINAL CUBE

1 UNIT

1 UNIT

*Is Minos right? If you do double the length of the side of the cube what happens to the volume and the surface area of the tomb?*

*Can you suggest what size the new cube should be if its volume is to be double that of the original altar of Apollo?*

# Paradoxes of Zeno

Zeno of Elea lived about 450 BC. He put forward 'arguments', which although they seemed logically sound, confused the mind and seemed to defy common sense. *How would you argue against Zeno's paradoxes?*

## Achilles and the tortoise

Achilles and a tortoise have a race. Achilles allows the tortoise to have a head start. They both start at the same time, but ... for every amount that Achilles moves forward, the tortoise must move forward as well. So when Achilles manages to reach the place where the tortoise was, the tortoise will have already moved on from there. This will continue indefinitely, so in this way Achilles will never be able to catch up with the tortoise.

## The arrow

Another of Zeno's paradoxes states that if you imagine an arrow flying through the air, then at any one particular instant the arrow must be in one particular place in space. (Especially as it cannot be in two places at once!) So if it is in this space at this instant, then it cannot be moving at all. This argument also holds for all other instants! In fact, you are just imagining that the arrow is moving.

# Chessboard problems

A chessboard is a square plane which has been divided into 64 squares by straight lines at right angles. The earliest boards which have been found were not chequered (black and white in alternate squares) ... this was a much later development which was introduced to help the players see the moves more easily. For example, the bishop which is only allowed to move along diagonal lines, keeps to the same colour which makes it easy to see which squares he might attack.

Why isn't the answer to the question above 64? If you start with a smaller sized board (a 3 x 3 board) and look carefully you will be able to see different sized squares.

## How many squares on a chessboard? No, not 64 ... nor 65 ...

*Try thinking about a 4 x 4 board next.*

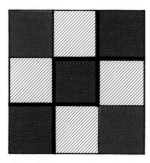

First of all it has 9 small squares ...
Then, 4 different overlapping larger squares...
Then there is also the outside square to add on.

When you have worked out how many squares there are on a chessboard (an 8 x 8 board), try to explain how you could work out how many squares there were on any sized square board.

*In how many different ways can you divide a chessboard into two equal parts of identical shape just by cutting along the lines between the squares?*

# Chequerboard divisions
You can look at this problem in a similar way to the previous one. *How many different ways can you divide a 2 x 2 board into two equal parts?* (Ways are only counted as different if you cannot reflect or reverse the pieces to get a way that you have already counted.) The answer is, one way, by cutting straight down the middle.

Now think about a 3 x 3 board. *What is the problem with all odd x odd bards?*

Here are three ways of dividing a 4 x 4 board.

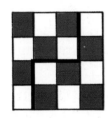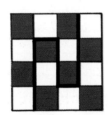

In fact there are six different ways of dividing a 4 x 4 board into two equal halves. *Can you find the other three ways? How many ways are there for a 6 x 6 board? ... an 8 x 8 board? ...*

# Odd x odd board divisions
You can tackle the odd x odd board problem by blocking out the centre square. Now the board has an even number of squares so you will be able to divide it into two equal halves. Remember that you may only cut along the lines. A 3 x 3 board has only one solution. *What about a 5 x 5 board, and a 7 x 7 board and so on?...*

# Lions and crowns

The women above is confronted with a cutting problem. She needs to cut the square piece of material into four equal parts and it is essential that each part should contain a lion and a crown. She also insists that the cuts can only be made along the lines drawn on the material. *Can you think of a way to do this so that each piece of material is exactly the same shape and size?*

# The golden chessboard
Below is an illustration of a golden chessboard. Set into the board are four red rubies. *Can you divide this precious board into four equal parts so that each part is the same shape and size and also contains a ruby?*

# Problem pieces

It has been shown that there are at least 197 299 ways of playing the first four moves in a game of chess – that is with each player making two moves. There are 71 782 different positions possible after playing the first four moves – 16 556 are possible when the players only move the pawns.

## The eight queen problem

One of the classic problems connected with the chessboard is finding a way to put eight queens on the board so that no queen can take any other queen. There are 92 different ways in which this can be done. One of the ways is shown below. *Can you find any of the other 91 ways?*

Another classic problem is to put five queens on a chessboard so that every square is 'commanded' by at least one queen. There are 4860 solutions to this problem. *How many different ones can you find? Can you find a way to place the five queens so that no queen is able to take any other queen?*

## Guarini's problem

One of the oldest problems in Europe connected with the chessboard was posed in 1512. On a board with nine squares, the two white knights have to change places with the two black knights (using knight's moves only). *What is the least number of moves which you need to do this?*

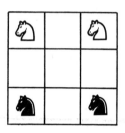

## Routes

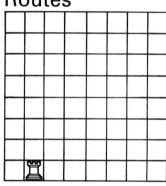

The rook starts in the square next to the bottom left. It must visit every square, once and once only, and finish in the top right hand square. *Can you find a route?*

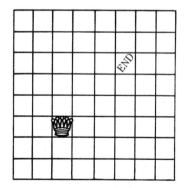

Move the queen to the end position in fifteen moves, visiting every square once and once only, so that she never crosses her own track.

## Getting started

Using one set of chess pieces and one chessboard, what is the maximum number of different ways of placing the pieces for the beginning of a game?

# Diophantine problems

## The life of Diophantus

The childhood of Diophantus was one-sixth of his life.

He grew a beard after one-twelfth more.

He married after one-seventh more.

Five years later his only child was born.

The child lived to half the age of the father.

Diophantus died four years after his daughter. *How long did Diophantus live?*

## Solving the problem

Diophantus of Alexandria was a Greek mathematician who lived in about 300 AD. He is best known for his collection of 189 problems and their solutions which he wrote in a book called *Arithmetica*. By using a form of algebra that was a mixture of words and symbols he was able to solve indeterminate (problems which have more than one solution,) and determinate equations (problems with only one solution). The problem above is said to have been written by a pupil of Diophantus. *Can you work out how long Diophantus lived?*

## One solution

Below are some determinate equations-that is they have just one solution. Can you solve them? The first two are quite easy but the third is hard.

> Find two numbers whose sum is 20 *and* the sum of their squares is 208.

> Find two numbers whose sum is ten *and* the sum of their cubes is 370.

> A farmer goes to market with 100 krona to spend. Cows cost 10 krona each, pigs cost 3 krona each and sheep cost half a krona each. The farmer buys from the cattle dealer, the pig dealer and the sheep dealer. He spends exactly 100 krona and buys exactly 100 animals. How many of each animal does he buy?

## Many solutions

The problem of Diophantus' life is a determinate equation and would probably not have interested Diophantus very much. Diphantus' fame lies in his invention of symbols to help him look logically at some mathematical problems and the solving of indeterminate equations (which are usually called Diophantine Equations). The following is an example:

If Sally has two more than three times as many pennies as Paula, how many does Sally have?

This problem has an infinite number of solutions ... if Paula had 5 pennies then Sally would have 17 pennies, if Paula had 6 pennies then Sally would have 20 pennies, if Paula had 7 pennies ...
Because there are an indeterminate number of solutions the best way to show the answer is in an algebraic form.

$x=3y+2$

Can you find a solution to the following Diophantine equation? Duncan is two years more than five times older than Eric. *How old is Duncan?*

# A Diophantine day

MELANIE KNEW THAT THE DAY WAS GOING TO BE SPECIAL... A MATHEMATICAL MYRIAD OF MYSTERIES!

It's a palindromic date today... 19/11/91... I wonder how many more palindromic dates there are this decade?

TUESDAY 19 NOVEMBE 91

BEFORE MELANIE HAD A CHANCE TO COME UP WITH AN ANSWER SHANTA AND SALLY ARRIVED FOR BREAKFAST.

Umm... that's interesting... do you know if we share out all the remaining slices of toast, equally between the three of us then there would be two slices of toast left over?

Well that's O.K. Tracey and Peter will be coming over soon, you can give them a piece each.

That wouldn't be fair... we should share the toast out equally between the five of us. And if we did that there would be four slices remaining.

JUST THEN TRACEY AND PETER ARRIVED...

You always think of everything mathematically, Melanie... How many slices of toast are there?

You'll have to work that one out for yourself Peter...

...and there's more than one answer to your question ... I might have more slices of bread which I could toast.

Where shall we go today?

I want to go to town to buy some wool. Why don't we all go?

ON THE WAY TO TOWN...

I've got a problem about going to a shop in France. I found it in an old algebra text book which was used by children in 1855.

What's the problem then?

First you need to know that one French Louis is worth 20 francs and 25 francs are worth one British pound...

Got that.

Imagine that you only have one pound coins in your pocket and the French shopkeeper only has Louis coins in her till. How can you pay for something that costs 45 francs, simply by paying with British pounds and getting French Louis coins back from the shopkeeper?

I like that problem because you can think about what would happen for different amounts of money. And which amounts of money are possible and which aren't.

Try something that cost £2.25

AFTER A MORNING IN TOWN THE FIVE WERE RETURNING HOME... THE PUZZLING CONTINUED...

...I've been looking at the prices of sweets in one of the shops.
I found that 3 small bars of chocolate and 1 bar of toffee cost as much as 1 packet of wine gums.
If 1 small bar of chocolate, 2 bars of chocolate and 3 packets of wine gums cost £1.25 how much did each thing cost?

Whilst you are figuring that one out... remember the wool I went to buy? Well I bought 2 different sorts. One sort cost 40p per ball and the other cost 55p per ball. I spent £15 altogether... so how many of each sort did I buy?

I knew today was going to be special. I think I call it a Diophantine Day.

WHY DID MALANIE CALL IT A DIOPHANTINE DAY?

# Weights and measures

Three robbers stole a jar containing 24 ounces of valuable balsam. Whilst making their escape they came upon a seller of containers, from whom they purchased three empty jars. When they reached their hiding place they decided to share out the balsam but found that their jars would only hold 5, 11 and 13 ounces respectively. *How could the valuable liquid be divided equally amongst the three by only using the four jars available?*

This problem is the first printed puzzle involving measuring liquids. It was posed by a sixteenth century mathematician, Niccola Fontana, who is more often referred to as Tartaglia. *Can you find a way to share the balsam which takes fewer pourings than your first try? Have you found how to do it with the least number of pourings?*

## 4 litres
You have a five-litre jug and a three litre jug and a supply of water. How can you measure exactly 4 litres? (Your are allowed to throw water away!)

## 8 litres
On the table are three jugs. The largest is full and contains 8 litres of wine. The other jugs are empty but can hold 5 litres and 3 litres respectively. The problem is to divide the wine so that there are 4 litres of wine in the eight-litre jug and 4 litres of wine in the five-litre jug. *What is the least number of pourings you need to do this if:*
*(a) you first pour wine into the five-litre jug?*
*(b) you first pour wine into the three-litre jug?*

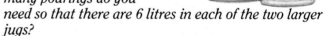

## 12 litres
Change the sizes of the jugs to 12, 7 and 5 litres. Starting with a full twelve litre jug of wine, *how many pourings do you need so that there are 6 litres in each of the two larger jugs?*

## 24 litres
This time start with a 24 litre jug full of wine and two empty jugs of 15 and 9 litre size. *How many pourings are needed now, if you want 12 litres in each of the two larger jugs?*

## Double orange
A litre carton of orange juice has all of its dimensions doubled. *How much orange juice would it hold?*

## A weighty problem

Another of Tartaglia's problems was to find the fewest number of weights needed to weigh any number of whole pounds between 1 and 40 *Can you find the answer?* (You may only put the weights on one side of the scales!)

In 1612, Claude-Gaspar Bachet, a French mathematician, published a book called *Problèmes plaisans et délectables* which contained many of Tartaglia's puzzles. It also contained two solutions to the previous problem. His first answer kept to the rules, but in the second one the weights were allowed on either side of the scales. *Can you find the least number of weights needed for this second problem?*

## Up to 121

If either side of the scales could be used only one extra weight would be needed to weigh any whole number of pounds between 1 and 121. *Can you work out what this extra weight is?*

*By adding yet another weight, what would be the maximum number of pounds which could now be weighed?*

## Numbers from India

Al Khowarizmi was an eminant Arab mathematician who lived in about 800 AD. He wrote many books about mathematics and one of these, called *Al'jabr* marked the beginnings of modern algebra. Another of his books, called *Arithemetic* described how the Indians wrote out their numbers, and also the way that they did their calculations. These numbers and methods caught on and spread across the Middle East. They became known in Europe in the twelfth century and later became the numbers and the ways of calculating that we use today.

## Alien messages

Is there intelligent life on other planets in other galaxies? If there is, how could we communicate with them? It would be highly unlikely that they would understand any of our written or spoken languages, but mathematics may provide the key. The following are diagrams of radio signals that could be beamed to outer space. Each line is a piece of mathematics. *Can you work out what they are?*

# Crossing the river

A woman arrived at a river bank. She had with her a basket of cabbages, a goat, and a wolf. Moored by the bank was a boat which would only carry the woman and one of the other three. If she takes the cabbages the wolf will eat the goat. If she takes the wolf the goat will eat the cabbages. *How can she get herself and all three safely to the other side of the river?*

Puzzles about crossing rivers seem to have first appeared in medieval times. The one about the woman, cabbages, goat and wolf is certainly very old. Tartaglia, a sixteenth-century Italian mathematician and Lucas, the nineteenth-century French mathematician who invented the Tower of Hanoi puzzle, both worked on various forms of this type of problem. The following are some variations — can you solve them?

## Mothers and daughters

Two mothers and two daughters were out walking. When they came to the river they saw that there was a shady bank on the opposite side which would be a much nicer place to picnic. Moored by the bank was a rowing boat. Unfortunately the boat was very small and could only carry the two daughters or one mother and one daughter. *What is the minimum number of crossings which they need to make so that they can all picnic on the shady bank?*

## More mothers ... more daughters

You might like to pose some other problems for yourself such as what is the minimum number of crossings need for two mothers and four daughters, or three mothers and two daughters or ...

The following puzzle can be found in a book of problems published in 1612. The book *Problèmes plaisans et délectables* was written by a French mathematician Claude-Gasper Bachet.

## Jealous husbands

Two wives and their husbands came to a river. Moored by the river was a rowing boat which would only hold two people at a time. However each husband is jealous and will not allow his wife to be with the other man, unless he himself is present. *How do the four people get to the other side?*

# More jealous husbands

Three wives and their husbands came to the same river and used the same boat to cross it. The conditions were the same as before. *How many crossings do they need to get to the other side?*

# Even more jealous husbands

If four or more wives and their husbands came to the river and were presented with the same conditions as in the previous two puzzles they would be unable to cross. However, if there was an island in the middle of the river the task does become possible. *Can you work out how?*

# Push and pull

Two engines each pulling two carriages meet on a single railway line. At the meeting point there is a spur of single line that has room for only one engine and one carriage. *How can the two trains pass each other?*

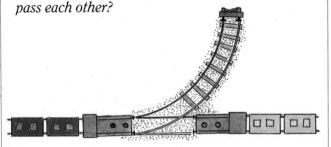

# Shunting

Here is a loop of railway. The two carriages X and Y are too tall to go under the bridge B. Can the positions of the two carriages be reversed by using engine E to push or pull them?

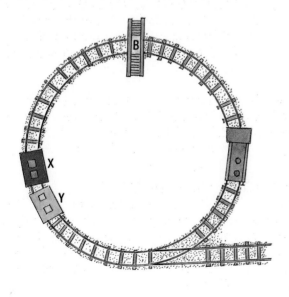

The king and his two children have been imprisoned at the top of a tall tower. Stone masons have been working on the tower and have left a pulley fixed at the top. Over the pulley runs a rope with a basket attached to either end. In the basket on the ground is a stone like the ones which were being used to build the tower. The stone weighs 35kg (75lb). The king works out that the stone can be used as a counterbalance - provided that the weight in either basket does not differ by more than 7kg (15lb). The king weighs 91kg (195lb), the princess weighs 49kg (105lb) and the prince weighs 42kg (90lb). *How can they all escape from the tower?* (They can throw the stone from the tower to the ground!)

# Three in a row

Tic-tac-toe has been played by many different peoples for thousands of years. Tic-tac-toe boards have been found carved on the walls of ancient Egyptian temples. The game was also played in China in 500 BC. The Romans played it as well. You can find tic-tac-toe boards in English cathedrals, which were carved into the seats by monks in the fourteenth century.

Tic-tac-toe is the oldest surviving game which is played by two opponents where no element of luck is used to determine the outcome. Other games of this sort include noughts and crosses, which is a development of tic-tac-toe, nim, draughts and its variations. It is possible to work out a strategy for all these games so that you never lose.

## Playing Tic-tac-toe

Below is a drawing of a tic-tac-toe board. The rules of the game are as follows: each player has a set of three counters, one set is white, the other is black. The players start by placing their counters alternately on vacant points of the board. When all the counters have been placed on the board play begins ... Each player, in turn, then moves one of their counters along a straight line to a neighbouring vacant point. The winner is the first player to get a line of three with their counters. *Which is the best point to put your counter on to start with? Does the player who goes first have an advantage over the other player? Is there always a winner?*

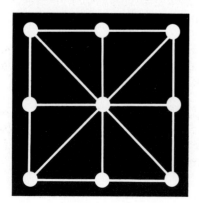

## First or second

In many games between two players the one who has the first move is considered to have an advantage. *Is this true in the following games?*

16 sticks are laid out in a line. A player may take 1 or 2 sticks away from the pile each turn. The player who takes the last stick is the winner. *Is it possible for the first or the second player to win all the time? Why?*

In this version of the game only 9 sticks are laid out. *Again, does it matter who goes first?*

**Rule change**
*What happens if the rule is changed so that the player who takes the last stick is the loser?*

*What number of sticks would the player who goes first choose if they wanted to win?*

*What number of sticks would the player who goes second choose to have if they wanted to win?*

# Nim

The game of nim probably came from China. It is a game for two players using three piles of sticks. This time each player takes 1 or 2 sticks away from any one pile in turn. *Is this game fairer for the first or the second player?*

## Take away more

The rules are changed so that instead of just allowing each player to take only 1 or 2 sticks, they are allowed to take 3, 4 or 5 sticks away. *Does this make a difference? What happens if there are more piles of sticks at the beginning of the game?*

# 3-D noughts and crosses

This game is a more difficult variation of 2-D noughts and crosses. To play it you will need to copy out the diagram below.

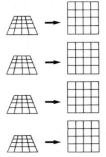

As in the 2-D version of noughts and crosses each player places their mark (the nought or the cross) in any vacant square on the grid. This time, you need to get a row of 4 noughts, or 4 crosses to win the game. The winning lines are more complicated as well, because they can be made both with straight and diagonal lines through the four boards, as well as the straight lines on any of the boards.

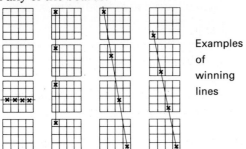

Examples of winning lines

# Counters

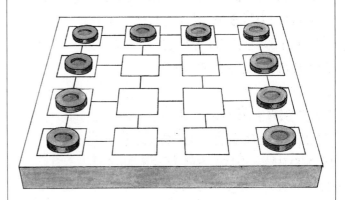

Above is a puzzle with counters. Counters can only move by making a vertical or horizontal jump over another counter. (Diagonal jumps are not allowed!) A 'jumped-over' counter is removed from the board. The idea of the puzzle is to take all but one counter off the board. In order to start you may move one counter into any unoccupied square.

# Reversing

1. Using draught-like moves (either sliding into a vacant square or jumping over one counter into a vacant space) reverse the order of the counters to 4, 3, 2, 1. *What is the smallest number of moves you need to do this?*

2. Add a seventh square and a sixth counter. *What is the smallest number of moves needed to reverse the order now?*

3. *If you had a strip of a million squares and 999 999 counters what would be the minimum number of moves needed to reverse the order?*

# Curiouser and curiouser

Alice was beginning to get very tired of sitting by her sister on the bank and of having nothing to do. Once or twice she had peeped into the book her sister was reading, but it had no pictures or conversation in it and what's the use of a book, thought Alice, without pictures or conversation?

This is how one of the most well read books in the world begins. It has now been translated into more than 46 different languages. *Alice's Adventures in Wonderland*, published in 1865, was written by Charles L. Dodgson, using the pen name Lewis Carroll.

Charles Dodgson, born in 1832, was destined to be a lover of puzzles, puns and conundrums. When he was a boy he became fascinated by puppetry and conjuring tricks. He used to entertain his family by putting on shows and he also produced magazines of puzzles and problems for his brothers and sisters. However, as a lecturer in mathematics at Oxford University he was said to be notoriously dull. Whilst at Oxford he wrote learned treatise which at the time were also thought to be boring and insignificant. Yet when Dodgson's imagination was set off on a whimsical exercise his genius shone; notably in *Alice*, which he began in 1865 as *Alice's Puzzle Book* and in *Through the Looking Glass*.

In the Wonderland book, Alice follows a white rabbit and in doing so manages to fall down a hole. As she falls down Alice begins to muse ... 'I wonder if I shall fall right through the earth? How funny it'll seem to come out among the people that walk with their heads downwards!'

## A hole through the earth

At many tea and dinner parties the Victorians would amuse themselves by setting each other puzzles to solve. The problem of what would happen if someone fell down a hole right through the earth was very popular during Charles Dodgson's time. *Would that person pop out on the other side?* The following are other puzzles that were also popular at the time.

## Eggs

Mrs Holly goes to market with a basket of eggs. On the way she meets Arnold the postman. She sells him half her eggs plus half an egg. Later she meets Ms Bakewell the teacher and sells her half of the remaining eggs plus half an egg. At the village pond she meets Charley, the local policewoman, to whom she sells half of the remaining eggs plus half an egg. Just before reaching the market Mrs Holly sells half of the remaining eggs plus half an egg to Denise, who delivers newspapers.

At the market, she sells half of the remaining eggs plus half an egg to Mr Early. She still has one egg in her basket. Throughout her five transactions she didn't break any eggs. *How many were in Mrs Holly's basket when she started out?*

> The problem of what would happen to someone who fell down a hole through the centre of the earth is very old. Galileo came up with our current theory in the seventeenth century, but the question still puzzled the Victorians. If someone were unfortunate enough to fall down such a hole they would fall with increasing speed until they reached the centre of the earth. After this their speed would decrease. The person would not fall out of the earth on the opposite side, but would fall back towards the centre. Gradually, due to the resistance, the person would come to rest at the centre of the earth.

## Clocks

A woman has two clocks. One clock gives the correct time only once a year. The other is correct twice a day. *Which is the better clock?*

## More clocks

A woman has two clocks. One clock lost a minute a day. The other clock didn't work at all. *Which is the better clock?*

## Sacks

Standing by the shop door were five sacks. Sacks A and B weighed 12kg. Sacks B and C weighed 13.5kg. Sacks C and D weighed 11.5kg. Sacks D and E weighed 8kg. Sacks A, C and E together weighed 16kg. *What was the weight of each sack?*

## The monkey and the weight

A frictionless pulley has been attached to a tower. Around the pulley is a rope. At one end of the rope there is a monkey, and at the other end there is a weight. The weight exactly counterweighs the monkey. *If the monkey began to climb the rope, what would happen to the weight?*

## An extra square

An 8 x 8 square is cut into four pieces. The pieces are then rearranged into a 5 x 13 rectangle.

8 x 8 = 64
5 x 13 = 65

*Where has the extra square come from?*

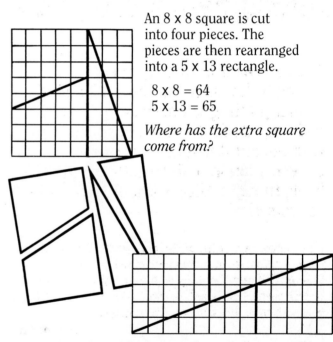

## Further escape

The problem on page 21, 'Escape from the tower', was probably invented by Lewis Carroll. Almost certainly the following addition to the puzzle is his.

Besides his two children the king also has a pig at the top of the tower which weighs 28kg (60lb), a dog which weighs 21kg (45lb) and a cat which weighs 14kg (30lb). There is an extra limitation that there must be one human at the top and bottom of the tower to put the animals in and out of the basket. *How can all six escape?*

# Sam Loyd

In a box are fifteen square tablets and there is a space for a sixteenth. The square tablets are numbered 1 to 15, in order, except for 14 and 15 which have been reversed as in the diagram. The tablets can slide horizontally or vertically one space at a time. The puzzle is to rearrange the tablets by sliding , so that all the numbers are in the correct order.

Sam Loyd offered a prize of $1000 to the person who could solve his 'fourteen-fifteen' puzzle. No one claimed the prize – the puzzle was impossible!

Sam Loyd (1841-1911) is perhaps America's greatest creator of puzzles. During his lifetime he is reputed to have made more than a million dollars from his inventive mind. He was devising puzzles before he was in his teens. When he was only seventeen he thought up the famous Donkey Puzzle. P.T.Barnum, owner of *The Greatest Show on Earth*, paid Sam Loyd ten thousand dollars to use it to advertise his show.

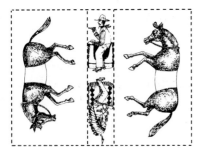

Trace this drawing. Cut along the dotted lines. *How can you fit the three pieces together so that both riders are correctly riding a horse?*

Below is one of Sam Loyd's most popular puzzles.

How many pieces of various sizes can you cut this pie into with six straight cuts?

## Inventing a puzzle

Sam Loyd was once asked what the mental process was for inventing puzzles. He replied that he wasn't quite sure but that the puzzles were all based on mathematics. He then went on to describe how one puzzle had come into his mind.

Sam was in the office of a pen manufacturer discussing with the owner the idea of offering some pens as prizes for his puzzles. During the course of a conversation, Sam persuaded the manufacturer to spend one thousand dollars on advertising in a puzzle magazine that he was starting up. Suddenly a puzzle popped into his head. Sam drew nine eggs and then said... 'What is the least number of straight lines needed to connect all nine eggs? The lines may pass through an egg twice and may cross.' The pen manufacturer thought it looked easy so Sam said, 'If you can solve it within an hour, I'll give you your thousand dollars of advertising free.' Alas, the manufacturer was unable to solve it.

O O O

O O O

O O O

*What is the least number of straight lines needed to join the nine eggs? Lines may cross and may go through an egg twice.*

# Henry Ernest Dudeney

Henry Ernest Dudeney was born in the English village of Mayfield in 1857. He became as famous in England for his puzzles as Sam Loyd was in America. The two were producing puzzles at much the same time. Although it is unlikely that Dudeney and Loyd ever met, they did write to each other and exchange ideas. The following are a small selection of the many puzzles invented by Dudeney.

## The Merchant's puzzle

One morning when they were on the road, the Knight and the Squire, who were riding beside the Merchant, reminded him that he had not yet propounded the puzzle that he owed the company. He thereupon said, "Be it so. Here then is a riddle in numbers that I will set before this merry company when next we do make a halt. There be thirty of us in all riding over the common this morn. Truly we may ride one and one, in what they do call single file, or in a column of twos, or threes, or fives, or sixes, or tens, or fifteens or all thirty in a row. In no other way may we ride so that there be no lack of equal number in the rows. Now a party of pilgrims were able to thus ride in as many as sixty-four ways. Prithee tell me how many there must perforce have been in the company."

The Merchant clearly required the smallest number of persons that could so ride in the sixty-four ways.

## Dividing three numbers

Find a number which will divide the numbers 480 608, 508 811 and 723 217 to leave exactly the same remainder in each case.

## The dispatch rider

A dispatch rider has to ride his horse from the rear of an army column to the general at the front. The army, which is forty miles long, advances forty miles whilst the rider gallops from the rear to the front. *How far has the dispatch rider travelled, if he also rides back to the rear again?*

## Triangle numbers

In his book *Amusements in Mathematics*, first published in 1917, Dudeney looks at triangle numbers...

These are numbers which can be represented by counters arranged as shown to form triangles. You may like to draw the next triangle numbers in the sequence ...

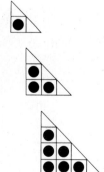

Dudeney also points out some other things about triangle numbers. For example, choose any number, times it by itself and add the original number. Halve the result and you will always get a triangle number. You might like to try it with some numbers...

$5 + (5 \times 5) = 30$ then half of 30 is 15
15 is a triangle number!

He also said that if you choose any number you will find that it is either a triangle number, or you will be able to make it by adding together two or three triangle numbers.

You might like to see if this works with a few numbers...

11 is made up of   10 + 1     (two triangle numbers)
12 is made up of   10 + 1 + 1(three triangle numbers)
           or         6 + 6     (two triangle numbers)
13 is made up of   10 + 3     (two triangle numbers)

*What else can you find out about triangle numbers yourself?*

# Chinese puzzle

The Chinese puzzle called the tangram is made from seven pieces cut from a single square. The five triangles, square and parallelogram can be used to make many different shapes resembling people, animals, objects and shapes.

Little is known of the origin of the tangram. It is probably very old, but the first mention of it in recorded history was in Chinese books printed about 1800. In his library Lewis Carroll had a book called *The Fashionable Chinese Puzzle*, which contained 323 tangram shapes. Though there is no date of publication, a note in the book states that the tangram was a popular pastime with Napolean whilst he was in exile. So we can assume that tangram puzzling was going on in Europe as early as 1820.

The American inventor of puzzles, Sam Loyd, claimed that the tangram was named after the legendary 'Great Tan of China', who was the first to cut the square into these seven pieces some four thousand years ago. Though a romantic thought, this is an unlikely origin of the name. The more likely story is that an American visiting China, having discovered the intriguing puzzle, used the Cantonese word for Chinese, *t'ang*, and the common European ending 'gram' to make up the word tangram.

## Making numbers
Make a set of tangram pieces. The numbers one to eight are shown below. *Can you make them using all seven pieces of the tangram for each number?*

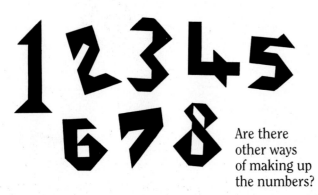

Are there other ways of making up the numbers?

## Squares with holes
Obviously you can make a square using all seven tangram pieces. You can make a slightly larger square with holes using the seven pieces as well. *Can you make the squares shown below? How many of your own 'square with holes' can you make?*

*Missing parallelogram?*

*Missing square?*

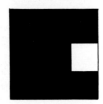

*Missing triangle?*

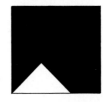

*Missing 'two triangles'?*

There are at least sixty different ways to make a square with two triangles missing. Here are some of the possibilities.

*How many more can you find?*

28

## Squares again
A square can be made with all seven tangram pieces ...

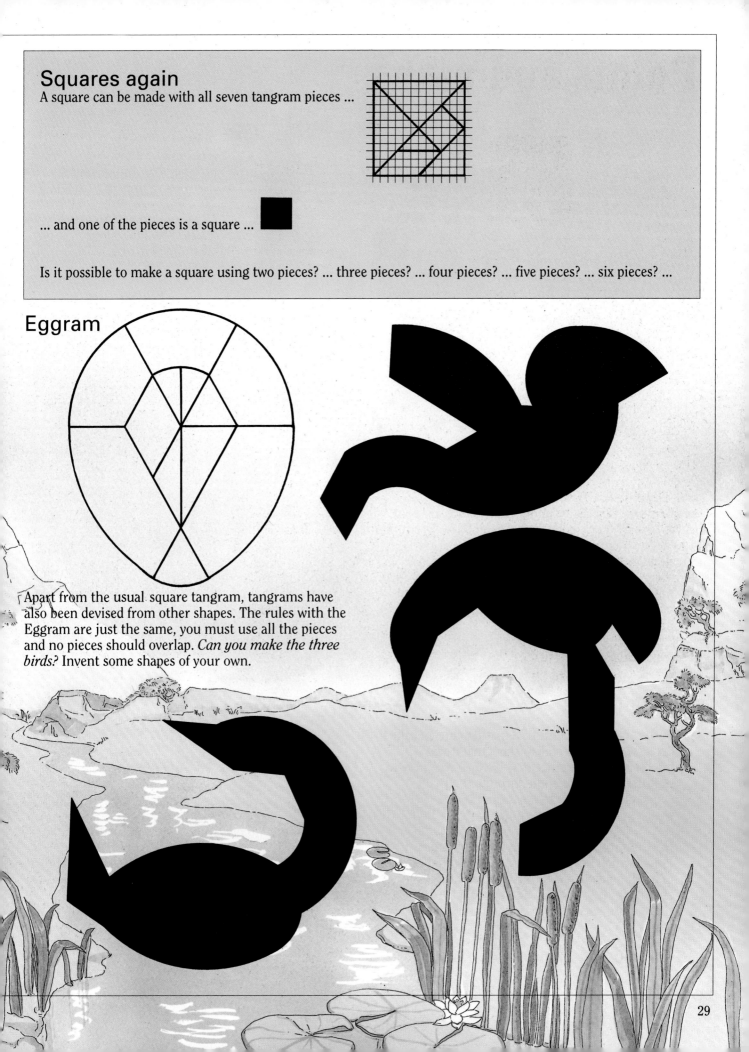

... and one of the pieces is a square ...

Is it possible to make a square using two pieces? ... three pieces? ... four pieces? ... five pieces? ... six pieces? ...

## Eggram

Apart from the usual square tangram, tangrams have also been devised from other shapes. The rules with the Eggram are just the same, you must use all the pieces and no pieces should overlap. *Can you make the three birds?* Invent some shapes of your own.

# Points and paths

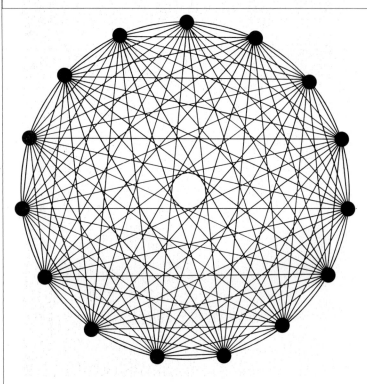

A three point mystic rose can be drawn with one continuous line.

Two continuous lines are needed to draw a four point mystic rose.

*What is the minimum number of continuous lines needed to draw the mystic roses below? (Remember, every point must be joined to every other point.)*

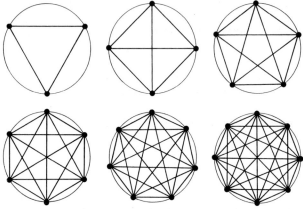

## Mystic roses

A mystic rose is made by joining dots which are equally spaced around a circle. Each dot is joined to every other dot with a straight line. In 1809, a mathematician called L. Poinsot raised the question: 'What are the minimum number of continuous lines needed to draw various mystic roses?' (A continuous line is one that is drawn without lifting the pen from the paper or retracing any on the lines.)

*Is it possible to predict the number of continuous lines for any mystic rose, no matter how many points it has?*

## The seven bridges of Königsberg

In the eighteenth century, a mathematician called Leonard Euler was able to show that it was impossible for the citizens of Königsberg, a town in Prussia, to find a route through their city which allowed them to cross each bridge over their river once and once only.

Here is a map of Königsberg showing the river Pregal which flows through the town, the island of Kneiphof which is in the middle of the river, and the seven bridges which the people of Königsberg tried to cross without retracing their steps.

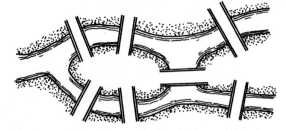

*Can your find a way to solve their problem?*

*What would happen if you were allowed to build a new bridge?*

Draw different rivers with different numbers of islands and bridges. Find out whether there is a route so that the bridges are crossed once and once only.

# Mathematical trees

Mathematical trees are grown with points and branches. The smallest tree possible has 2 points and 1 branch.

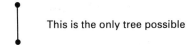

This is the only tree possible

The next size tree has 3 points and 2 branches.

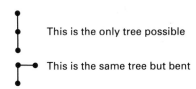

This is the only tree possible

This is the same tree but bent

With 4 points and 3 branches there are two possibilities.

How many trees are there for 5 points and 4 branches?... 6 points and 5 branches?... 7 points and ?...

*How will you make sure that your trees are definitely different?*

# Spider and solids

Can the spider walk along all the edges of the tetrahedra in one continuous walk without retracing its path?

With the same condition can the spider walk around the edges of the polyhedra below?

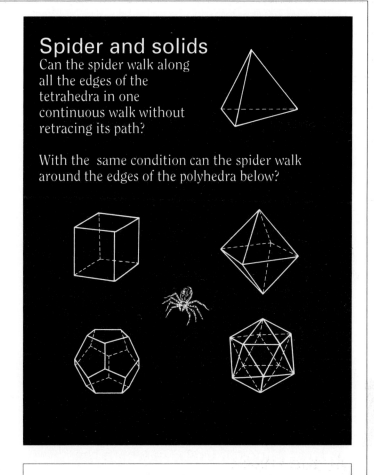

# An elephant eating buns

The drawing below is a map of an elephant house. In each room there is a bun. An elephant wants to eat all the buns without visiting any room twice. *Is it possible? If the elephant wanted to eat the least number of buns, which route should it take? What would happen if the doors were opened and closed in different ways?*

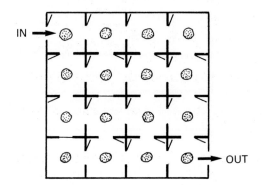

Investigate elephant houses with different numbers of rooms.

# Sprouts

Sprouts is a game for two players. Dots are drawn, well apart, on a sheet of paper. The numbers of dots determines how long the game will last. Six or seven dots gives a good game. In turn, each player draws a line joining one dot to another, or a dot to itself. The player then places a dot wherever they choose along the line they have drawn. The second player does the same as the first player and so on.

**Rules for sprouts**
- A dot can only have a maximum of three lines leaving it. (If a line joins a dot to itself this counts as two leaving lines.)
- A line cannot cross itself or any other line.

**Winning sprouts**
The player who is the last one able to draw a line is the winner.

The winning line

# Lost in thought

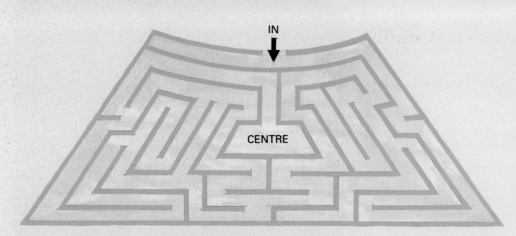

## A problem in topology

One way of ensuring that you reach the centre of a maze, is to place a hand on the right hand wall. Keep your hand on that wall and don't follow any other paths that would cause you to remove it. *Is it possible to design a maze where this wouldn't help you?*

It is not known who created the first maze. Mazes have been found all over the world. They have been carved in stone, cut into earth and drawn on cave walls. Perhaps the most famous maze was the Labyrinth, which was designed and built by Daedalus for King Minos of Crete, in which the legendary minotaur was kept.

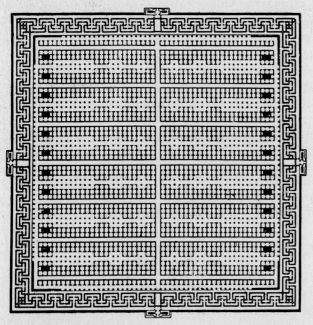

The illustration above shows a plan of one of the earliest mazes. It was built in Ancient Egypt about 4000 years ago. Although the site is known, the actual maze has disappeared over the centuries. It was said to have contained over 3000 rooms. Whether the maze was made for the purpose of creating secret meeting places, or as part of a tomb, or something else entirely, is not known.

## Designing a maze

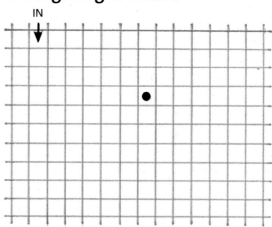

Start with a piece of squared paper. Mark an entrance point and an exit or other goal.

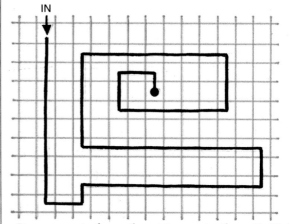

Draw a route from the entrance to the exit. Make it complicated!

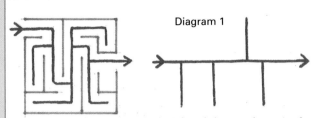

Diagram 1

Topologists call the maze on the left and the one above *simply connected*. The route in a *simply connected* maze can be stretched out into a straight line with the false routes as straight lines off it at right angles (see diagram 1).

Topologists call the maze on the right *multiply connected*. Try the right hand system to get to the goal. Does it work? Try turning it into a diagram like the one above. *Can it be done?*

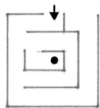

IN

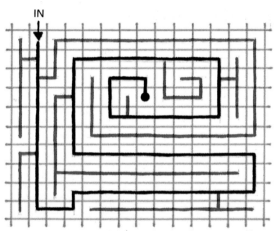

Now draw some false paths leading away from the main path. Make sure that there is a path going through every square.

IN

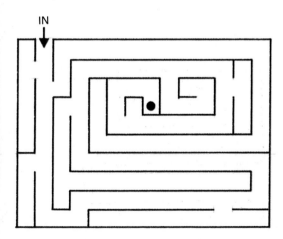

The last stage is to take a piece of tracing paper and draw in the walls of the maze. the walls are the lines of the squared paper which have not been crossed by a path.

# Number maze

IN

| 1 | 6 | 5 | 2 | 1 | 1 | 2 | 1 | 2 | 1 | 2 | 3 | 4 | 1 | 2 |
|---|---|---|---|---|---|---|---|---|---|---|---|---|---|---|
| 2 | 3 | 4 | 3 | 5 | 1 | 2 | 1 | 2 | 3 | 1 | 1 | 1 | 4 | 3 |
| 5 | 4 | 2 | 3 | 4 | 2 | 1 | 1 | 1 | 1 | 1 | 2 | 5 | 5 | 1 |
| 6 | 7 | 1 | 4 | 3 | 2 | 1 | 3 | 2 | 2 | 5 | 3 | 6 | 2 | 2 |
| 2 | 1 | 1 | 3 | 1 | 3 | 1 | 5 | 1 | 3 | 4 | 5 | 7 | 1 | 3 |
| 3 | 3 | 2 | 2 | 5 | 4 | 3 | 2 | 1 | 4 | 3 | 6 | 6 | 5 | 4 |
| 4 | 4 | 5 | 1 | 1 | 5 | 6 | 7 | 8 | 1 | 2 | 7 | 3 | 4 | 5 |
| 5 | 2 | 1 | 2 | 2 | 2 | 1 | 7 | 6 | 5 | 4 | 2 | 2 | 1 | 6 |
| 6 | 6 | 5 | 4 | 3 | 4 | 5 | 6 | 1 | 2 | 3 | 1 | 2 | 2 | 1 |
| 7 | 1 | 4 | 5 | 2 | 1 | 2 | 3 | 4 | 5 | 6 | 8 | 2 | 3 | 4 |
| 8 | 2 | 3 | 7 | 6 | 5 | 4 | 3 | 2 | 1 | 2 | 7 | 6 | 6 | 5 |
| 1 | 2 | 4 | 5 | 1 | 2 | 3 | 4 | 5 | 1 | 1 | 3 | 5 | 6 | 6 |
| 2 | 3 | 4 | 6 | 7 | 1 | 2 | 3 | 4 | 5 | 6 | 3 | 4 | 3 | 2 |
| 5 | 4 | 3 | 2 | 4 | 3 | 2 | 9 | 8 | 4 | 7 | 2 | 1 | 2 | 1 |
| 6 | 5 | 1 | 1 | 2 | 3 | 1 | 2 | 7 | 6 | 8 | 1 | 2 | 5 | 7 |
| 7 | 6 | 2 | 4 | 6 | 4 | 5 | 3 | 6 | 5 | 1 | 2 | 3 | 4 | 5 |
| 8 | 7 | 8 | 2 | 3 | 1 | 2 | 4 | 9 | 4 | 4 | 2 | 1 | 7 | 6 |
| 4 | 5 | 9 | 1 | 8 | 7 | 6 | 5 | 8 | 3 | 2 | 1 | 9 | 8 | 3 |
| 3 | 2 | 1 | 6 | 5 | 4 | 3 | 6 | 7 | 4 | 4 | 3 | 2 | 1 | 2 |
| 4 | 3 | 2 | 7 | 3 | 9 | 8 | 7 | 6 | 5 | 6 | 7 | 8 | 9 | 1 |
| 5 | 6 | 7 | 8 | 9 | 10 | 9 | 8 | 7 | 8 | 9 | 10 | 6 | 5 | 1 |

OUT

Can you find a route from the top to the bottom of the maze. You may only move horizontally or vertically – no diagonal moves are allowed. The route must go 1; 1, 2; 1, 2, 3; 1, 2, 3, 4; 1, 2, 3, 4, 5; and so on.

## Other mazes

Try creating different types of mazes. Use special sequences of numbers like in the maze above, or try to make ones based on shapes. Use different grids as a base. Always start by drawing a complicated route from start to finish. Make complicated false routes, not just at the start, but also from the finish as well, because many people try to solve mazes by tracing back from the finish.

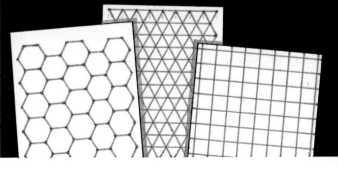

# Curious squares

The magic square below was found in Khajuraho, India. Although it is not the earliest magic square, it does date back to the twelfth century.

| 7 | 12 | 1 | 14 |
|---|----|---|----|
| 2 | 13 | 8 | 11 |
| 16 | 3 | 10 | 5 |
| 9 | 6 | 15 | 4 |

## What is a magic square?

The simplest type of magic square is an arrangement of numbers on a grid of cells that form a square. The numbers in the square should be placed so that the rows, columns and two main diagonals all sum to the same total. The numbers used in a real magic square must be the same as the number of cells in the square, e.g. a 3 x 3 square has the numbers 1 to 9 in it; a 4 x 4 square has 1 to 16; a 5 x 5 square has 1 to 25; and so on.

| 52 | 61 | 4 | 13 | 20 | 29 | 36 | 45 |
|----|----|---|----|----|----|----|----|
| 14 | 3 | 62 | 51 | 46 | 35 | 30 | 19 |
| 53 | 60 | 5 | 12 | 21 | 28 | 37 | 44 |
| 11 | 6 | 59 | 54 | 43 | 38 | 27 | 22 |
| 55 | 58 | 7 | 10 | 23 | 26 | 39 | 42 |
| 9 | 8 | 57 | 56 | 41 | 40 | 25 | 24 |
| 50 | 63 | 2 | 15 | 18 | 31 | 34 | 47 |
| 16 | 1 | 64 | 49 | 48 | 33 | 32 | 17 |

## Franklin's square

In about 1750, Benjamin Franklin constructed the square above. The numbers 1 to 64 (8 x 8) are used to construct it. All the rows and columns add up to 260. But there are also some other curious discoveries to be made...

- Add the numbers in either half in any row. What is the total? Add the numbers in either half of any column. What is the total?
- What is the total if you add up the four corner numbers and add it to the sum of the four middle numbers?
- If you add up the bent diagonals (A to A etc., as shown in the diagram) on Franklin's square, what totals do you get?
- Add up any block of four cells. What totals do you get?

*Are there any other curious properties in the square?*

## The first magic square

Constructing magic squares has been an amusement for many centuries. Originally they were thought to have mystical qualities. The drawing below is called the Loh-shu. It first made its appearance in China in about 2800 BC. Can you see why it is a magic square of the order 3?

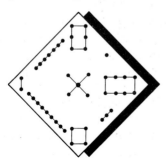

## Euler's square

| 1 | 48 | 31 | 50 | 33 | 16 | 63 | 18 |
|---|----|----|----|----|----|----|----|
| 30 | 51 | 46 | 3 | 62 | 19 | 14 | 35 |
| 47 | 2 | 49 | 32 | 15 | 34 | 17 | 64 |
| 52 | 29 | 4 | 45 | 20 | 61 | 36 | 13 |
| 5 | 44 | 25 | 56 | 9 | 40 | 21 | 60 |
| 28 | 53 | 8 | 41 | 24 | 57 | 12 | 37 |
| 43 | 6 | 55 | 26 | 39 | 10 | 59 | 22 |
| 54 | 27 | 42 | 7 | 58 | 23 | 38 | 11 |

The curious square above was constructed by the eighteenth-century Swiss mathematician Leonard Euler. Why is it not a magic square? Can you find any interesting properties in it? If you place a knight on the top left cell, you can land on all the numbers 1 to 64, in numerical order, by making knight's moves between them.

# Magic tracing

The patterns below were drawn by tracing over magic squares in numerical order.

Tracing over the Loh-shu

Tracing over Franklin's square

Tracing over Euler's square

*What different patterns can you find with other magic squares? Try tracing just odd or just even numbers.*

## Talisman square

This is a Talisman square with a constant of 1...

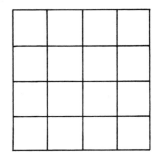

... because if you look at any one number in the square and then find the difference with each of its neighbours, this 'difference' is greater than 1.

*Can you put the numbers 1 to 16 onto this grid to make a Talisman square with a constant of 2 (all the differences greater than 2)?*

*Is it possible to use the numbers 1 to 16 to make a square with a constant of 3?*

Try Talisman squares of different sizes.

## Making odd squares

The following is a method for creating a magic square of the order 3. Always start by putting the 1 in the middle cell of the top row, then place the rest of the numbers (2 to 9) by making an upward diagonal move to the right. If you come out at the top of the column return on the bottom. If the cell is occupied, put the number directly under the last number you placed. Try this method for a 5 x 5 square. Does it work for a 7 x 7 square? Will it work for any odd numbered square?

## Modest indeed

When she taught the king to play chess, he was so pleased that he said she could have any reward she wished. She thought for a moment and then said: 'I am a modest creature, so I'll go for a modest reward. Just place one gold coin on the first square of the chessboard for me, then double on the next and then double that on the next, and so on, until there's a pile on every square'. *Do you think this was a modest reward?*

# Colourful puzzles

In 1976 Kenneth Appel and Wolfgang Haken proved that you need a maximum of four colours on a map so that the colour of any two regions next to each other are different.

Some maps can be coloured by using less than four colours. Try the following...

Take a sheet of paper and draw straight lines from one side of the paper to the opposite side. *What is the minimum number of colours you need to colour a map such as this?*

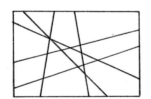

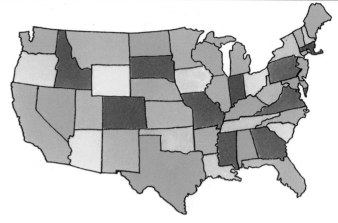

Only 4 colours are needed to colour in this map of the USA so that no two states next to each other are the same colour. *Is it possible to use fewer colours?*

## Colourful solids

If a map is drawn on a sphere, what is the minimum number of colours needed for all situations?

Imagine a map drawn on a Möbius strip. Will four colours be enough to make sure that regions next to each other do not have the same colour?

## Colouring edges

Imagine that you have drawn a network ...

and that you want to colour the edges on the network so that each touching edge is a different colour to the next.

*What is the smallest number of colours you can use for this network so that you keep to the rule?*

Draw different networks and see how many colours you need for each one. *Can you predict how many colours you will need for different types of networks.*

*If you were to colour the edges of a cube so that each touching edge is a different colour, what is the minimum number of colours you need?*

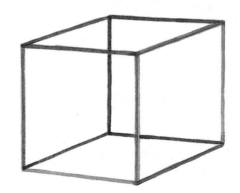

# Colourful board

Draw a 5 x 5 board and take 25 counters - five counters each of five different colours. Take the first colour, say green, and place all the counters so that there are no two green counters in a horizontal, vertical or diagonal line with each other.

Fill the whole board with the 25 counters in this way so that there are never two counters of the same colour in a line with each other.

If this is difficult, start with a 4 x 4 board with 16 counters. (You will need four each of four different colours.)

# Making up colourful problems

Below are the nets for four cubes. Copy them, cut them out and colour them as shown. Then make them into cubes.

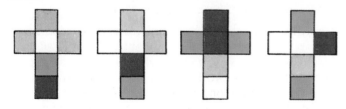

Now arrange the four cubes into a tower so that on each side of the tower all four colours are shown. Invent some similar problems.

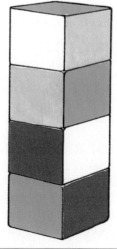

# Colour cube

Paint 27 small cubes nine different colours (three cubes painted in each colour). Build a 3 x 3 x 3 cube so that there is only one of each colour showing on each side of the cube.

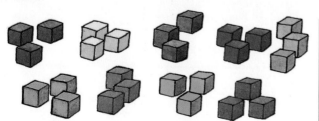

# Colourful doors

Every door in a street has a number painted on it. All the odd numbers are painted blue and all the even numbers are painted yellow. *If you add a blue number to a yellow number what colour do you get?*

# Liars, hats and logic

THIS SQUARE IS BLANK

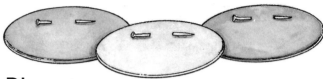

## Discs

A man and a woman were sitting in a room. A third person entered the room and said, 'Here are three discs, two blue and one red. I shall pin one disc on each of your backs and put the third one in my pocket without either of you seeing its colour. You will then be able to see the disc on each other's back. The first one who can tell me the colour of the disc pinned to their back shall receive the prize.'

The man looked at the disc on the woman's back but remained silent. The woman then knew the colour of her disc and she claimed the prize. *What was the colour of her disc and how did she know?*

## Logical paradoxes
In the sixth century BC, Epimenides made the following statement:

'All Cretans are liars.'

Epimenides was a Cretan. *Can you see the problem with his statement?*

*Which of the following two statements below is true?*

> THE SENTENCE BELOW IS TRUE.

> THE SENTENCE ABOVE IS FALSE.

## Five hats
Three women sat in a row, one behind the other. All three were blindfolded. 'Here are five hats,' said a fourth woman, 'two green hats and three yellow. I shall place one hat on each of your heads and put the other two hats into the cupboard. You may then remove your blindfolds. But, you must remain seated and you cannot turn your head. The one who can tell me what colour hat she is wearing will receive a prize.' The fourth woman then put the hats on and put the other two into

## A woman, a child and a tiger.
A mother and her child were out working in the field. Suddenly a tiger appeared and took hold of the child. 'Give me back my child,' pleaded the woman. 'I will,' replied the tiger, 'if you can correctly predict the fate of your child - either that I eat him or I give back to you unharmed.' 'You will eat him' said the woman'. *What do you think was the fate of the child?*

## More about hats

*How many different combinations of hats to heads are possible with five hats and three women?*

*How many different combinations of hats to heads are possible with seven hats and three women? ... Nine hats? ... Eleven hats? ...*

## Red and green hats

Three men and one woman were sitting facing each other. All were blindfolded. A fifth person announced that she would place either a red or a green hat on each of them. They should then remove their blindfolds and if they saw a red hat then they should stand on their chair. If they could correctly state the colour of their own hat they should stand on the table.

Only red hats were put on the four heads. When the blindfolds were removed, all four stood on their chairs. After a while the woman climbed onto the table. *How did she work out the colour of her hat?*

the cupboard.
The woman at the back of the row removed her blindfold and saw the two hats in front of her, but she remained silent. The woman in the middle removed her blindfold and saw one hat. She also remained silent. The woman at the front of the row did not remove her blindfold, nevertheless she correctly stated the colour of her own hat and claimed the prize. *Can you work out the colour of her hat? How did she know?*

## Who got what?

Six of the children who lived in a road shared the same birthday though they were all born in different years. Can you work out, from the following information, the age of each child and which of the three types of birthday gift they received?

1  Alan and the five year old got a paint box.

2  Ellen and the 6 year old each got a set of colouring pencils.

3  Both the 7 year old and the 8 year old got felt-tipped pens.

4  Betty and Fred go to a different school to the 7 year old, whose hobby is stamp collecting.

5  Betty, who will be 9 years old on her next birthday, and the 5 year old are shorter than Charlie.

6  The 9 year old has red hair, unlike Charlie.

7  The 10 year old likes ice cream and is taller than Charlie.

8  Charlie got felt-tipped pens and one of the other boys got a set of colouring pencils.

9  Alan is not as tall as Charlie.

To help solve the 'Who got what?' problem it may be useful to draw a grid like this.

| NAME | 5 | 6 | 7 | 8 | 9 | 10 | GIFT |
|------|---|---|---|---|---|----|------|
| A    |   |   |   |   |   |    |      |
| B    |   |   |   |   |   |    |      |
| C    |   |   |   |   |   |    |      |
| D    |   |   |   |   |   |    |      |
| E    |   |   |   |   |   |    |      |
| F    |   |   |   |   |   |    |      |

# Terces pot

**TELEGRAM**

THE SUPPLY OF GAME FOR LONDON IS GOING STEADILY UP HEAD-KEEPER HUDSON WE BELIEVE HAS NOW BEEN TOLD TO RECEIVE ALL ORDERS FOR FLY-PAPER, AND FOR PRESERVATION OF YOUR HEN PHEASANT'S LIFE

The telegram above comes from the beginning of the Sherlock Holmes story, *The Gloria Scott*. It needs to be looked at carefully to decipher the real message which is contained within it. Read the first word and then every following third word of the telegram.

This kind of coded sentence is not easy to create. Try to make up some of your own messages using this rule. Also try to make up some more coded sentences by changing the rule so that you read every fourth, or every fifth word.

## Colourful Code

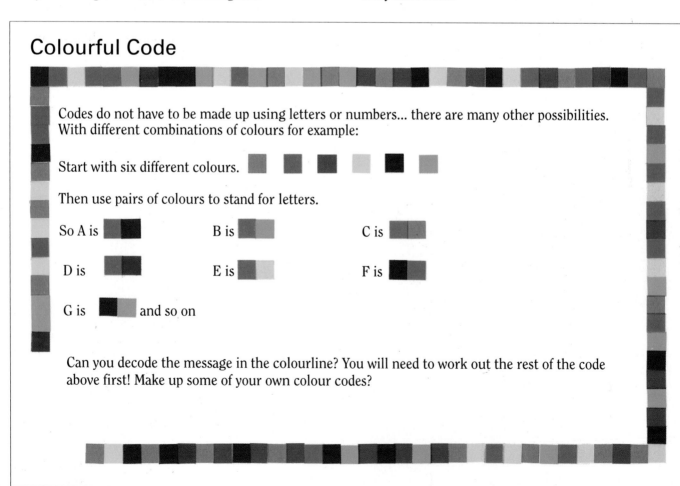

Codes do not have to be made up using letters or numbers... there are many other possibilities. With different combinations of colours for example:

Start with six different colours.

Then use pairs of colours to stand for letters.

So A is            B is            C is

D is            E is            F is

G is       and so on

Can you decode the message in the colourline? You will need to work out the rest of the code above first! Make up some of your own colour codes?

## Dancing code

In another story, Sherlock Holmes brings a group of gangsters to justice when he cracks their secret code which uses dancing stick men to stand for letters. The figures below are not the sames as the figures which Holmes decoded, but he used the following information and good guesswork to crack the code.

E is the most commonly used letter in written English. After E the letters which are used most often are T, A, O and I – then N, S, H, R and L in that order.

## A cracking good code

TIG SRWDVJ OO TIG
HZRRXJTBAN IT
ERWDP TP TIG SVO
OG TIG SRWDVJY
OO TIG OUJHV TXQ
SJFHW

*Can you decode the message above?* Here are some clues to help your.

1  The first letter of each word is not in code.
2  Right angled triangles of letters are used to put each word into code.
3  The following diagram shows you how to put the word SQUARE into code...

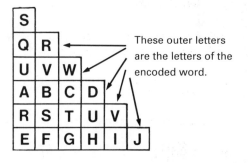

These outer letters are the letters of the encoded word.

## Pig pen

The pig pen code was very popular with Union prisoners during the American civil war. *Can you work out the message by using the clue on the right?*

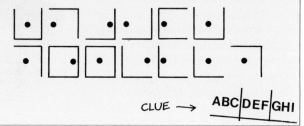

CLUE →  A B C | D E F | G H I

# Sets and spots

A double six set of dominos contains 28 pieces. How many dominoes in a double five set...? a double seven set...?

How many spots are there in a double six set of dominoes? A double five set?

Around the edge of this page is an incomplete set of dominoes. Which set is it? Which one is missing?

A double six set of dominoes consists of different tiles, each with a pair of spots, except for the blanks. On the right are the 28 tiles which would make up the double six set. Unfortunately some have been left blank. Can you work out which are missing?

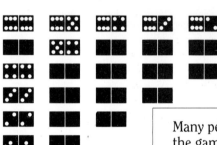

Many people will be familiar with the game of dominoes, which is normally played with a double six set. There are many interesting puzzles which can be explored using the domino pieces.

This group of dominoes consists of all the dominoes from a set whose spots add up to six. Investigate other groups which are made up of spots which add up to other totals.

Here are two groups of dominoes. Each group has a total of eight spots. What is the largest group with a total of ten spots? Investigate different sets of dominoes for different totals of spots.

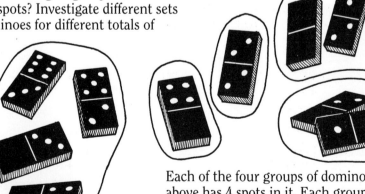

The group of dominoes on the right consists of dominoes where the difference between the half tiles is always 3. Are there any more? Investigate other differences.

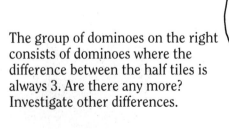

Each of the four groups of dominoes above has 4 spots in it. Each group consists of different dominoes. How many groups are there which add up to 5 spots, 6 spots...? Investigate!

# Cards, matches and dice

## Cards...

Use the cards from Ace (one) to nine from one suit. Shuffle the cards and lay them out in 3 rows of 3.

*The idea is to move the cards so that they are in descending order from nine to one.*

The rules are that you may only move a card onto another card if it is of a higher value. Only one card may be moved at a time.

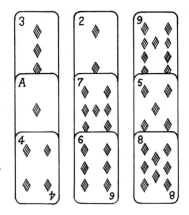

## Playing card year

How many spots are there in a pack of cards?

How many cards in a pack?

How many picture cards in a pack?

How many suits?

## ... matches...

Use 10 matches.

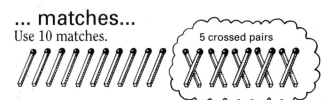

5 crossed pairs

The idea is to move the matches so that they are in pairs.

The rules are that you must jump over exactly two matches when moving. You may only move one match at a time.

*How many different ways can you find for solving the problem?*

Use 15 matches.

Move the matches into sets of three. The rules are that you must jump over exactly three matches when moving. You may move only one match at a time.

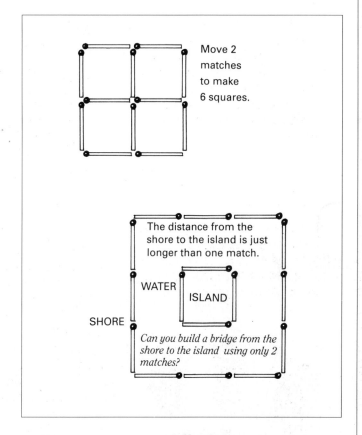

Move 2 matches to make 6 squares.

The distance from the shore to the island is just longer than one match.

WATER    ISLAND

SHORE

*Can you build a bridge from the shore to the island using only 2 matches?*

## ... and dice

How many different ways are there of putting the numbers 1 to 6 on a dice?

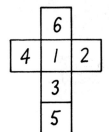

How many different ways are there of putting the numbers 1 to 6 on the dice if the numbers on opposite sides add up to seven? What do you usually find on a dice?

# Puzzling cubes

To solve the Rubik Cube puzzle by trial and error would be a daunting task. There are over 43 000 000 000 000 000 000 possible arrangements of the little cubes.

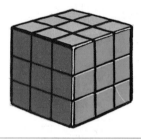 

## Rubik's Cube

Perhaps the biggest puzzle craze of this half of the century is that of the Rubik Cube. First developed in Hungary in the 1970s by Erno Rubik, it was in plentiful supply across the world as millions of children and adults twisted it around trying to get the cube back to its original state.

At first glance a Rubik Cube appears to be a simple 3 x 3 x 3 cube with each of the six 3 x 3 outside faces a different colour. But once in your hand you find that the columns and rows can be twisted horizontally or vertically.

To do the Rubik Cube puzzle you first twist columns and rows in a haphazard way until all of the six faces are multicoloured. To solve the puzzle you must return the cube to its original state (i.e. a single colour on each of the six faces). With over 43 000 000 000 000 000 000 possible arrangements this is no easy task. It would be impossible to do it simply by trial and error. The easiest way is to take the cube apart, admire the simple but extremely clever construction that makes the movements of the cube possible and then to replace the parts so that the faces are their original colour.

## Colour the cube

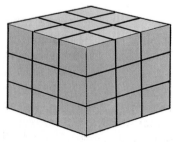

If you put 27 blocks of wood together to make a cube and then paint the outside orange...

How many blocks of wood will have just one side painted orange?
... 2 sides painted orange? ... 3 sides painted orange... 0 sides painted orange?

What if you put 64 blocks together and painted the outside orange?

What about 125 blocks ... 216 ...?

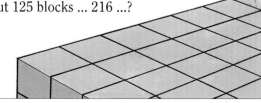

# Cube routes

A
B

The diagram above represents the skeleton of a building constructed with girders. A construction worker wanted to get from A to B by either
- walking along horizontal girders or climbing down vertical girders, (without going backwards or
- upwards in direction) *How many possible routes are there?*

*Report*

From Ms. Jones Chief Inspector
I was inspecting the scales of Brown's shop on the main street. I discovered that the shop was using dishonest scales — one arm was longer than the other.
LONGER →

When I put 3 circular weights on the long arm they balance with 8 cube weights on the short arm. When I put one cube on the long arm it balanced six circular weights on the other arm. The true weight of a circular weight is 10 grams.

*What is the weight of a cube?*

## The Soma cube

Can the seven pieces above be fitted together to form a solid 3 x 3 cube? The answer is yes! In fact there are more than 230 different ways - not counting reflections or rotations - to put the cube together. The seven pieces were devised by Piet Hien in Denmark. He originally visualised the puzzle in his mind during a lecture, and later made up a set by sticking wooden blocks together. *How many different ways can you find of making the cube?* The shape below is made using all seven Soma pieces. *Can you construct it?* Devise some shapes of your own.

## An investigation with cubes

Look at the seven pieces that make up the Soma Cube. One piece is made from three cubes. The other six pieces are made by putting together four cubes. *How many different arrangements are there of five cubes, six cubes....?*

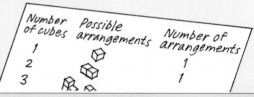

| Number of cubes | Possible arrangements | Number of arrangements |
|---|---|---|
| 1 | | 1 |
| 2 | | 1 |
| 3 | | 1 |

These shapes are made using four cubes. They are mirror images of each other. They are counted as different shapes because it is impossible to turn one over and get the other shape.

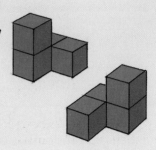

45

# A few solutions

**Page 5**  *A few keys*  All the numbers between 1 and 50 can be made using only the six keys shown.

**Page 7**  *Problem 79* 16807 measures of flour
*P.S. to problem 79* One

**Page 8**  *Silver and sisters*  2 shekels 36 grains

**Page 9**  *Measuring land*

The other two are quite difficult. Look at the shape that they finish up as. Try to imagine how the orignial shape could be cut up to make them.

**Page 10**  *The Delian Problem*  If the side lengths double, the area increases 4 times and the volume increases 8 times.

**Page 11**  *The Arrow*  Time is continuous and moving just as the arrow is moving. A particular instant in time passes and cannot be recaptured. So even if an arrow is stationary it is moving through time! In this case it is better to think of the arrow moving through the air and not to consider the time element.

**Page 12**  *How many squares on a chessboard?*  204 squares.

**Page 13**  *Lions and crowns*
This is one of the four identical shapes. Can you work out how they fit together and where the crowns and lions go?

*The golden chessboard*
This is one of the four indentical shapes. Can you work out how they fit together and where the jewels go?

**Page 14**  *Routes*

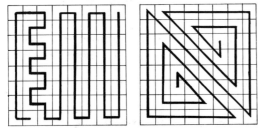

**Page 15**  *The life of Diophantus*  Diophantus lived to the age of 84 years.

**Page 18**  *4 litres*

**Page 20**  *Cabbages, goat and wolf*

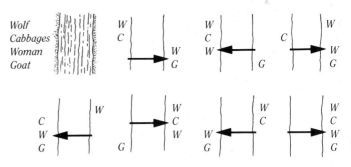

**Page 24**  *Eggs* Mrs Holly started out with 63 eggs
*Sacks* A weighs 5.5 kgs, B weighs 6.5 kgs, C weighs 7kgs, D weighs 4.5 kgs, E weighs 3.5 kgs.

**Page 26**

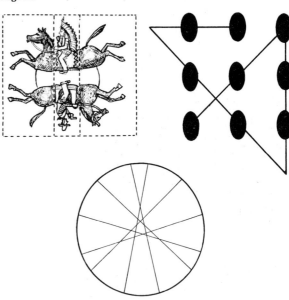

**Page 28**

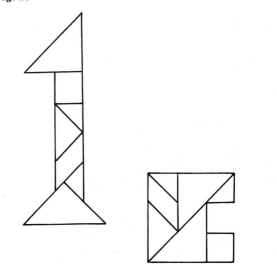

**Page 29**

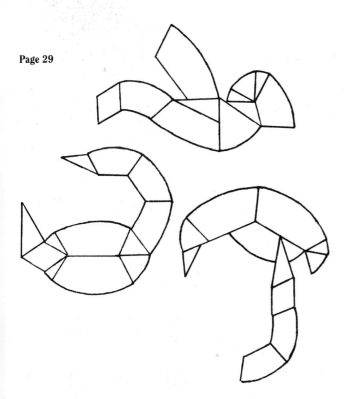

**Page 31**  *An elephant eating buns.*

Are there other ways?

**Page 33**

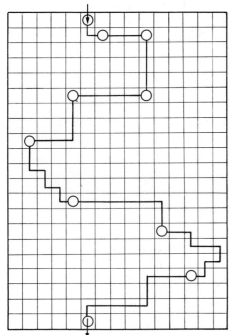

**Page 35**  *Talisman Square*

| 13 | 3 | 16 | 5 |
|----|---|----|----|
| 10 | 7 | 11 | 2 |
| 14 | 1 | 15 | 8 |
| 6 | 9 | 4 | 12 |

Every difference between any number next door to each other is *greater* than 2.

**Page 37**  *Colourful doors* Blue

**Page 38**  *Discs*

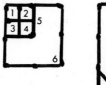  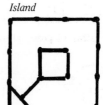  

**Page 39**  *Who got what?*

Alan, 9 years, paint box
Betty, 8 years, felt-tipped pens
Charlie, 7 years, felt-tipped pens
D (not named), 5 years, paint box
Ellen, 10 years, colouring pencils
Fred, 6 years, colouring pencils

**Page 40**  *Telegram messsage*  THE GAME IS UP
HUDSON HAS TOLD ALL
FLY FOR YOUR LIFE

*Colourful code*  THIS IS AN INTERESTING CODE
BECAUSE IT IS MORE LIKE A PATTERN

**Page 41**  *Pig pen*  ESCAPE TONIGHT

**Page 43**  *6 squares*  *Island*

**Page 45**  *Cube routes* Start with a 1 x 1 x 1 cube. How many routes are there?

*Cubes* Cube weight 15 grams

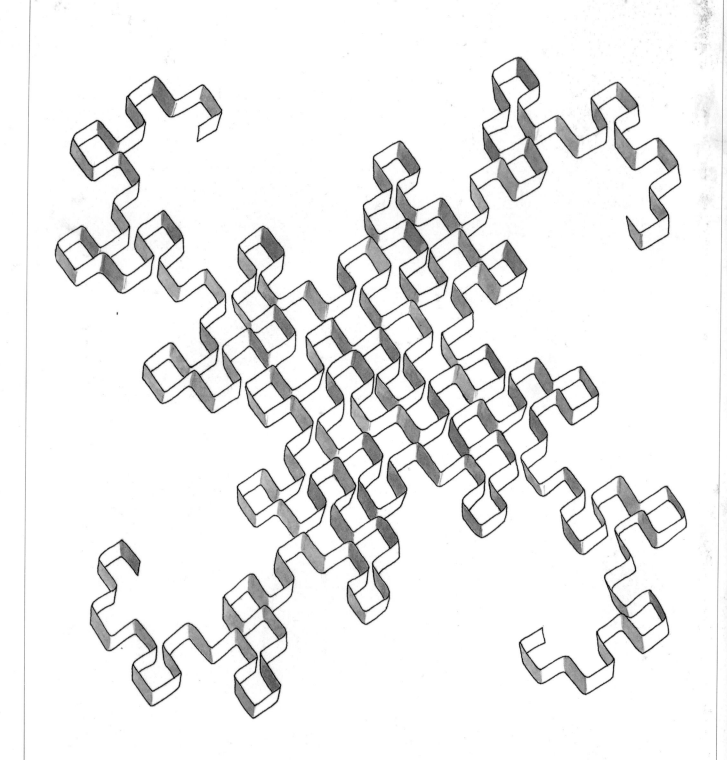